Kakalambalala

by Jan Mogensen

Crocodile Books, USA

An imprint of Interlink Publishing Group, Inc.
NEW YORK

First American edition published in 1993 by

Crocodile Books, USA
An imprint of Interlink Publishing Group, Inc.
99 Seventh Avenue • Brooklyn, New York 11215

Published simultaneously in Danish by Høst & Søns
Forlag, Copenhagen.

Library of Congress Cataloging-in-Publication Data

Mogensen, Jan.
   Kakalambalala an African tale / retold and illustrated
by Jan Mogensen – 1st American ed.
      p.   cm.
   Summary: The starving creatures of the savannah first
send the swiftest animal, then the strongest, and finally the
most powerful to the mountain to learn the name of great
magic tree but they all fail.

   ISBN 1-56656-136-1
   [1. Folklore – Africa.] I. Title.
PZ8.1.M699Kak 1993
398.21–dc20
[E]   93-2910
                                             CIP
                                             AC

Printed and bound in Belgium

Long ago in Africa, there was a time when no rain had fallen for days and weeks and months. The animals had no water to drink and no food to eat. They were starving.

When things were at their worst, the animals set out for a great tree that stood in the heart of the savannah. They had been told it was a magic tree, and that if anyone stood under it and called it by name, the tree would give them all the fruit they could eat.

But the animals still had a problem. No one knew the tree's name.

Then the lion, who was king of the beasts, stepped forward and said: "Many years ago my grandfather told me that a great spirit who lives up on the mountaintop knows the magic tree's name. Let us send the fastest of all animals to the mountain spirit so we can quickly learn the tree's name."

At this moment the turtle stepped forward. "I know I am not the fastest," she said, "but I would like to go up the mountain."

The other animals began howling and roaring and grumbling. "How," laughed the hyena, "will the slowest and dumbest of us get something to eat in a hurry?"

And then, without further debate, the animals chose to send the hare.

Early the next morning the hare set out on her journey. She ran with great pleasure, jumping over hill and dale, zigzagging up the steep mountain. She only stopped when she stood before the great spirit on the mountaintop.

"Oh, mighty spirit," said the hare, "tell me the name of the magic tree, because all the animals are dying from hunger."

"The name is *"Kakalambalala,"* answered the mountain spirit. "Hurry back and don't forget it."

The hare sped down the mountain. And when she was almost down she thought, "No other animal could have run as fast as I have. In a moment I'll be back, and we will all eat to our heart's content."

CRASH!! At that moment the hare, who had been lost in her own thoughts, ran smack into a big termite mound that stood in the middle of the trail. She could hardly get up. She was dizzy and faint. But finally she started running again, very shakily.

When the hare arrived back on the savannah, the animals all shouted excitedly, "What's it called? What's it called?"

"The tree's name is *Kaka – Kaka – Kaka ....*" But the hare could not remember.
The termite mound had knocked her memory clear out of her head.

The animals were furious. Hunger rumbled in their stomachs. They howled and roared and grumbled. Then the lion stepped forward and said, "We must choose another animal to get the magic tree's name. Let it be the strongest of us all."

When the lion had spoken, the turtle stepped forward again. But now the animals were so upset that they didn't even allow her to speak. The rhinoceros threatened to trample her flat as a pancake if she even opened her mouth. In the end they all agreed to send the buffalo.

Early the next morning the buffalo set out on his journey. As he rumbled along, the ground shook. He looked neither to the right nor to the left. He only stopped when he stood before the great spirit on the mountaintop.

"Oh, mighty spirit," said the buffalo, "the hare forgot the name. Tell me, because the animals are dying from hunger."

"The name is *Kakalambalala*," answered the mountain spirit. "Hurry back and don't forget it."

The buffalo thundered down the mountain, his hooves sending up sparks. And when he was almost down he thought, "I might not be as fast as the hare, but I am big and strong, and nothing can stop me. In a moment I will be back, and then we'll all eat until we burst."

CRASH!! The buffalo ran full speed into the termite mound. He stood completely still. The ground swayed beneath him, and stars floated before his eyes. He stood like that a long time. Then he slowly began to stumble forward in a daze.

When he arrived back on the savannah, the animals all shouted excitedly, "What's it called? What's it called?"

"The tree's name is *Kaka -- Kaka -- Kaka ....*" But the buffalo could not remember. The termite mound had knocked his memory right out of his head.

The animals were becoming desperate. Their insides were screaming with hunger. They howled and roared and grumbled. The turtle tried to say something but only got kicked by the giraffe.

At last they all agreed that the lion should go. For if even the king of beasts could not bring the name back, then who?

Early the next morning the lion set out on his journey. In huge leaps and bounds he quickly climbed the steep mountain and only stopped when he stood before the great spirit on the mountaintop.

"Oh, mighty spirit," said the lion, "the hare and the buffalo have forgotten the name. Tell me, because the animals are dying of hunger."

"The name is *Kakalambalala,*" answered the mountain spirit. "Hurry back and don't forget it."

The lion raced down the mountain at a dizzying pace. And when he was almost down, he thought, "The hare is fast, and the buffalo is strong, but I am powerful, and nobody dares stop me. In a moment I'll be back, and we shall feast upon mountains of food."

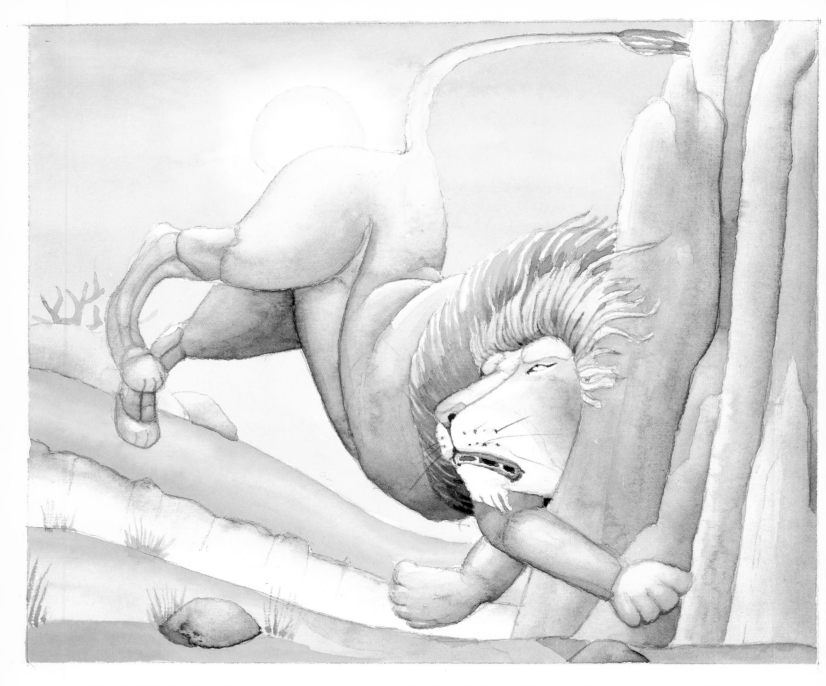

CRASH!! The lion hit the termite mound with his full force. He could hardly breathe. He didn't know who he was, or where he was. He stood like that a long time. Then slowly he came to himself, shook his mane, and continued on in a daze.

The animals stared at the lion in breathless anticipation when he came walking back. The lion stopped. He wrinkled his big forehead and opened his mouth: *"Kaka – Kaka – Kaka ...."* But even the lion could not remember the name. The termite mound had knocked his memory completely out of his head.

The animals were without hope. Hunger stole their strength, and they waited to die. Now the turtle stepped forward again and said, "I would like to go up to the mountain spirit and get the name." The animals stared at her. How was the lowly turtle to do what the lion, the buffalo, and the hare had been unable to do? But nobody had a better idea, so they let her go.

Early the next morning the turtle set out on her journey. She set one foot in front of the other and crawled slowly and cautiously up the steep mountain. She crawled and didn't stop until she stood in front of the great spirit on the mountaintop.

"Another animal!" shouted the mountain spirit with great irritation. "Couldn't even the lion remember the magic tree's name?"

"No," answered the turtle.

"Well, then listen carefully," said the mountain spirit, "because this is the last time I will say it. The name is *Kakalambalala*."

"Kakalambalala," said the turtle as she left the mountaintop.
And *"Kakalambalala,"* said the turtle when she was a little way down.

"Kakalambalala," said the turtle when she was halfway down.
And *"Kakalambalala,"* said the turtle when she was almost down.

"*Kakalambalala*," said the turtle when she saw the huge termite mound in the middle of the trail.

And "*Kakalambalala*," said the turtle as she carefully walked around the termite mound.

It was night when the turtle finally returned.

"Well, turtle," said the animals. "Did you get the name?"

But the turtle didn't answer them. She walked straight past them and went to the foot of the magic tree. She stopped there and said very slowly and very clearly: *"Kakalambalala."*

Instantly huge, juicy fruits rained down from the magic tree. The animals threw themselves on the fruit and ate until they were exhausted. There were mountains of food, and there were even some leftovers for the turtle.

Every day the turtle stood under the magic tree and said its name, and every day fruit poured down. After a long time, the rain came again. The savannah was rich and green, and the animals went their separate ways.

But never again did the hare, the buffalo, the lion, or any of the other animals laugh at the slow turtle.